Hope runs through it

Hope runs through it

poems by

M.W. MacKay

FOUR SQUARE PRESS
BOSTON, MASSACHUSETTS

Library of Congress Control Number: 2012948415

ISBN: 978-0-9851689-0-2

Table of Contents

Hope runs through it

Boardwalk
Plum Island, Massachusetts

There's music in the wood
a rounded reverb
a muffled twang
of vibrating planks
a wooden xylophone
that draws me forward
to play my way
to the next bend.

How graceful a thing
to follow a path
that sings
that floats
through pitch pine and salt marsh
to hear cordgrass whisper
as it trails through my fingers
to feel the wind hum
as it slips through my hair
to receive the bright silence
of late winter sun.

Sweet things
For Billy Collins

You sit at the dentist's waiting
for your cleaning reading
a library book unfolding
the dog-eared corners wondering

what it was about *this* poem
that made someone mark it as special.
You want to mark them all
small miracles of composition and wit

read them aloud and share their charm
hand them out like hard candies
you find in your pocket
gift-wrapped in crinkly cellophane

ready to offer the next passerby
or the woman waiting next to you.
But she has her head down
engrossed in her own book.

And you are, after all, at the dentist's
where they frown on sweets.

Moon shadow

Frozen globe floats low
bathes the earth in cool silver
casts my moon shadow.

Mother's Day

You weren't much more
than two months old.
I held you like a china doll.
You weren't quite real
weren't quite mine.
Then you gave me
your first smile
and I signed on for life.

Oldsquaws
Madaket beach
Late December

Pencil flicks, dashed off
fluttering commas against a raspberry sky
hundreds, thousands, of oldsquaws
gossips all
calling back and forth
as they stream northeast
to roost for the night.
I eavesdrop on the chatter
that drifts down like snow
faint, beautiful, incomprehensible.

I wish I spoke duck.

Grandmother hands

I remember
tracing the map of veins
following the line of blue
to rough knuckles
thumbing the worn skin
feeling you gentle my hands in yours.

I remember
watching your fingers fly
sliding your needle through corduroy
creating from whole cloth
my jumper, deep red
a cotton giraffe
peeking out from the pocket.

I remember
sensing the surety
of your hands guiding mine
chopping, slicing, stirring
as we made Chicken Marengo
falling under the spell of your rough voice
weaving the tale of Napoleon's chef
foraging in the French countryside.

I remember
hearing the whisper of your palm
smoothing my pillow
loving your fingertip kiss on my brow
as I slipped toward sleep.

Panic attacks

The monster's got us
in a death grip.
It strangles my son
my innocent one
chokes out reason
shoves in panic
until, drowning,
my son grabs me.
I can't breathe
and we both sink down.

Germ phobia

He washes his hands until
the sink drips foam,
the floor is a lake,
and his wrists turn raw red.

When I wash later,
in defiance,
I rub my fingers
in the leftover soap film
that coats the sink
so I won't waste any more than
we've already lost.

Breathing room
Polpis Moors, late fall

It's empty now, the summer people gone.
There's space to spare, to walk the moors alone
To watch a hawk's slow drift, and wander on
And feel the silence seep into my bones.

I sense here still the ghosts of early fall
The moors awash in red, the fading green
The sharp shriek of a barn owl's hunting call
The sound, the scent, the color of that scene.

Now silvered brown takes hold, the green withdrawn.
Bare branches let the land's soft curve show through
Reveal the cool gray of a kettle pond
And frame the distant ocean's vivid blue.

I reach out wide, this beauty to embrace
And breathe in Autumn's parting gift of grace.

Appetite
Madaket beach

Monster waves romp, white manes streaming
whipped to frenzy by screaming winds
wild things, all froth and fury
gobble sand dunes, chomp at clay cliffs
rip out tree roots, grind up roads
topple houses, gulp them down
roar their hunger, scrabble for more.

I lean into the gale to watch the sea rage
slit my eyes against the sand's sting
think *it's not personal* as a gust grabs my hat.

But as I watch my island gnawed to nothing
swallowed piecemeal by insatiable hunger
I'm terrified.

Bittersweet

You get used to the bitter
around the edges
always there.
You make yourself swallow
an alphabet soup of
504, IEP, SPED
ADHD, OCD, NVLD
with a side of short bus.
You choke down
a nasty casserole of
disastrous play dates
unreturned phone calls
salted with misery and silence.
You want to vomit up
the defeat that sits
like a stone in your gut
as you watch your boy
slouched in darkness
wrapped in loneliness
lit by his laptop's ghost glow.

You long to savor
something sweeter
to balance the bitter.
You wonder
what normal tastes like.

Picturing you
To Jesse

Your picture haunts me
caught in a photoclip next to my desk.
You're three, maybe four
leaning out your castle window
blue eyes wide under
your blueberry hat (my favorite)
head tilted, like your smile
so happy, so pleased, so proud
of your plastic palace.

This morning, years later
you struggle
as you do each day
to battle the demon
that lurks by the sink
that attacks, right on schedule
that knows your weakness
that hisses its lies:
Wash more, you're filthy
you'll never be clean.

You look so weary
as you fall into your chair
and ask for my help.
"You're clean," I tell you
knowing I shouldn't get caught in the battle

that my words reinforce the cycle of washing.
You turn with a sigh
pull your cereal bowl close
and lose yourself in the comics.

Then your dad arrives home
from his morning bike ride
with a treat, just for you
from Starbuck's, your favorite.
You're surprised, you're pleased
your eyes widen: "Really? For me?"
And that sweet, crooked smile
breaks through the clouds
a picture I'll keep for years to come.

Time to pray

Make time to pray my pastor preached.

Stop worrying the world like a dog
with a chew toy and unclench your jaw.

Let up on the gas pedal pull off
the racetrack and exit the vehicle.

Turn off your IPod tune out
the TV and drop in to silence.

You choose the catch phrase.

But it's hellishly hard to summon stillness
with Doubting Thomas as your spirit guide.

Respite

He grabs his backpack
snatches his lunch
kicks my seat
with adolescent fury
squawks his misery
storms and slams
out of the car.

In whirlwind's wake
silence settles like dust.

I feel relief.

Six hours of respite
to gather my wits
brace myself for
the afternoon onslaught
of fits and anxiety.

I pull in the driveway
rest head on hands
and drip tears.

Fade to black

Madaket beach, winter

Trees turn gray
berries bleed color.
My hands grow ghostly
in front of my face.
I watch amazed as
the world's leached of light.

All to fire
the fat bright
glowing growing
vibrant screaming
fuchsia streaking
across the sky.

The sun slides down in a raspberry shriek
flame snuffed out in the icy ocean
drowning the day in black.

Crisis center

I wanted to write
from the center of the crisis.
Nothing resolved
no uplifting ending.
Just a psych unit with
scuffed, cracked floors
bare mustard walls
a near-empty room
foam mattress
sheets that don't fit
no cords, no strings
no belts, no shoelaces
nothing dangerous here.
Just locked windows
locked doors
locks and
locks and
locks.

We arrive each day
follow narrow
hospital corridors
that snake between
claustrophobic walls.
We call in
tap on the window
and wait

silent, empty
for entrance
for permission
to see our child.

There he stands
limp black hoodie
(no strings)
sagging jeans
(no belt)
bare feet
(no shoelaces)
waiting
waiting
to open the floodgate.

How could you lock me in here?
You idiots!
You don't know what to do with me,
so, what, you just dump me?
Do you think I'm crazy, like them?
They belong here, but I'm fine.
I'm fine.
I'm fine.
Get me out.
Get me home.
Bring me home.
Now.
Please.

I tried to write
from the center of the crisis.
But I had no words.

Bargaining for Jesse

You can have my voice. I'll stop singing.
Silence.
And my words. I won't write anymore.
Darkness.
What else?

Not him. I can't give up one for the other.
Empty.
I'll take it on. Give it to me instead of him.
Nothing.
Anything you want. Anything.
No answer.
You won't bargain, will you?

I'll take silence as a "no."

Intelligent design

Wavelets glide in, lick my feet
hiss back over gleaming wet pebbles
litter the beach with countless treasures.
I feel one tumble over my foot.
The ocean has coughed up another gift.
I pick up the moon shell
all spirals and swirls
absently slide my thumb into
its slick inner curve where
creamy pink blushes into rose
a thing perfect in form and function.

I pitch it back.
It splashes, vanishes
marked only by ripples
that dance outward
silvered by sunlight
until balance returns
and nothing remains
but the smooth, rhythmic
rolling of the wavelets.
Harmony of Nature
form, function, balance.

Cloying
sentimental
bullshit.

Is that why a child
smart, beautiful, kind to his core
has a brain that misfires
spirals out of control
hurls him into panic?
Imbalance
built into his system.
Check your design
and try again.

Focus

I focus out
on what could be
what should be
to other children
healthy, normal
nothing in their way.

You blur, fade out
lost behind my vision
of "should" and "could."

You nudge me, insistent
slide across the couch
lean your shoulder into mine.
I'm here, your body reminds me.
See me.

I pull back my distant stare
and focus.

Sideways
To my husband

You say you look at him sideways
when the anxiety explodes.
The full-on view would knock you flat
and crush you with its brutality.

You ask me what I do
when he wails for me with a cry
that sends a shock through my body.

I tell you we're not alone,
we all have burdens to bear,
a cliché born of truth
as we feel our backs crack
under our particular cross.

I tell you to look straight at him,
at the fat that covers his once-slim frame,
a side effect of the drug
that helps keep anxiety at bay,
at the water that soaks his pants, waist to knee,
from obsessive washing
in his fight to feel clean,
at his face, his eyes shifting,
trying to meet your eyes,
trying to connect.

Look straight at him.
See what lies hidden
gifts, beautiful ones
searching for a way out
in his drawing, his music
his often astonishing words.
And see his bravery
as he faces each day
with a cross that dwarfs ours.

Winter's tale

Shoveled, melted, cleared at last.
Firm footing, easy driving.
Nothing left but stray ice mounds
stubbornly clinging to curbs.
The earth can breathe again
and I smell Spring.

But the Old Man's
not done yet.
A flake drifts down
settles on my hair.
Another alights
cool on my cheek.

And more, more…
floating, whirling
swirling, drifting
spinning madly in
smoky gusts
coating my jacket
frosting the earth
slathering snow
on sidewalk and street.

Winter claims full rights
from solstice to equinox
putting my plans on ice.

Last refuge

You sit together
in Burger King
last refuge of the old
the homeless
the mentally ill

You pick at your fries
he abandons his lunch
wanders to the window
headphones draped
round his neck
cord trailing

He watches seagulls
fight for scraps
in the near-empty lot

You stare at his profile
halo of curls
glasses slipped down
to the tip of his nose
a shadow figure limned
by harsh winter light

You see his potential
your bright beautiful child

You see hidden damage
brutally crippling as
blindness deafness missing limbs

You picture him in thirty years
same glasses thinner hair
when you can't save him
can't shelter him

When he's made this
his last refuge

In Advent

I hunger for light.
Not the junk-food bright
glare that blazes from malls
and screams back the dark
with extended Holiday hours.

But the soft, silent flicker
of a single candle
a kiss of light
to caress the dark
a breath of peace
to soothe black despair
a whisper of hope
to feed my soul
and show me the way.

Gatekeeper needed

Shut up, shut up, shut up!
echoes in my head
even as the gaffe
slips past my lips.

I need a gatekeeper
with a sharp ear
who slams my mouth shut
before the blunder spills out.
Not this lazy oaf
who dozes off
when I need him most.

So now the word's out
the secret spilled
the gossip repeated
the stupid jibe thrown.

Can I eat my words, please
with a side of discretion
take a vow of short silences
to think first, then speak
and hire a gatekeeper
with a caffeine addiction?

Work in progress

I work hard on him
correct, improve
tweak, fix
show him how to do it right.
Pencil in politeness
insert discipline
erase anxiety.
As if I had something to do with it.
As if I could write him myself.

Then he breaks out
dances a ridiculous hip-hop
twirls, bounces, windmills
around the living room
adolescent whirling dervish
in sweatshirt and jeans
singing some divinely inspired
nonsense that's funny as hell.

Where did *that* come from?

Not me.

Prayer

Lord, teach me to pray.
If I ever knew how
I don't anymore.
I doubt You profoundly
and find emptiness
where You're supposed to be.

Lord, breathe on the embers
of my belief
and stir them to life
so my words can fly up
and find You.

Lord, send me a sign
a clear one I can't mistake
(and I am good at mistakes)
that You haven't left us
that You Are.

Lord, give me the faith
of the holy ones
who find You, somehow
even when You're buried
in a mountain of despair.

Lord, help me in my unbelief
for I ache to pray.

Mother's heart

To my mother

For where your treasure is,
there will your heart be also.
—Luke 12:34

I've done nothing
to deserve it except
offer my resentment

at paying your bills
cooking your meals
helping you dress.

I don't want to mother
no longer be daughter.
But care must happen.

So I run your shower
test the water on my arm.

Just the right warmth
to rinse your hair.

You close your eyes
sigh with pleasure.

I tuck you in
as you once did me.

Your sudden, fierce hug
throws me off-balance.

Unwanted burden turns
to heart-stopping gift—
my benediction.

You can quote me

All the world's a stage
and all the men and women merely players.
But my son has yet to pick up his script.
And forget about his exit;
He refuses to make an entrance.

Two roads diverged in a yellow wood.
My boy sat down at the crossroad
and diverted himself with *Angry Birds*.

Consider the lilies of the field
how they grow
they toil not
neither do they spin.
Just like my kid.

All's fair in love (and war).
So if I love him,
can I lie, cheat, and trick him
into getting off his ass and
doing something with his life?

Patch work
Tuesday morning Bible study

I go in broken
looking for solace.
Lend my arm to a friend
whose legs no longer work right.
Find a woman waiting
who's been treated like trash
most of her life.
Admire her latest artwork
a transformation
of tin scraps, broken brooches
folded, spindled, mutilated punch cards
that makes trash talk.
All the regulars.
Each with our broken.
All with our grace.

Lord, let our crazy glue
of loss pain love support
patch us together
for another week.

Sanctuary
For my husband

My rock.
I hold you tight
feel you tremble from the pounding
uncaring, unrelenting wave
after wave.
Still, you plant your feet
and stand fast.

My anchor.
I rely on you
as the storm screams
as our ship whips wildly
as I feel us slip
then feel you catch, yet again
and hold us fast.

My sanctuary.
I rest in you
when the winds back down
their shrieks turned to muttering
and there you are, steadfast
to hold me, calm me, make me laugh
and remember love.

Threads

The simple life eludes me.
A myth, a fairy tale
Cinderella for grownups.
A sweet dream of peace
that leaves me longing.

God hands me
a tangled knot.
I pick at it, tease it
try to smooth out the mangles
and feel for the lifeline
with clumsy fingers.

But, like all great artists
God adds new twists, new ties
a baffling pattern
beyond my understanding.

A thing of beauty
or a mess of snapped threads?

Winter's grip

Snow blankets all the island, lying deep
In drifts of blinding white on dingy sand.
Ice claims the ocean as it outward creeps
To still Nantucket Sound and trap the land.

Our feet crunch snow, the sharp sound out of place
In air so silent cold, so pure and bright.
We stop, then move on at a gentler pace
Into a world made strange, into the white.

We walk, my son and I, toward the sea.
The snow drifts high, then higher in our way.
We struggle through until we both break free
To see the ocean, frozen, mute, and gray.

The ghostly beauty touches us with awe.
We look our fill, then quietly withdraw.

Easter Sunday land

My friend tells me
in poor countries
the church is packed
on Good Friday
but on Easter
it's empty.
And their cross isn't bare.
It holds a man
twisted in pain
nails thrust through his hands, his feet.
A sufferer, like them.

Is that why I find You
in the ache and tears
of Good Friday
but, by Easter morning
You're gone?
Can we only find You
when we're stripped bare
no comfort left
but another hand, clutching ours?

So how do we find You
in this Easter Sunday land
that won't walk the path
through the heart of Good Friday
that won't reach out
to grasp the hands
of those who know You best?

Summer dreams

I dream of summer, days of sand and heat
Of ocean, cool beneath the breathless air.
The water sooths my burning, sand-scorched feet
And trickles down my skin, drips off my hair.

I dream of beach grass dancing in the breeze
A rippling wash of green against the white.
I walk through, and it tickles at my knees.
I touch a slick-sharp blade and feel its bite.

I dream of wandering, aimless, on the beach
A lazy search for shells along the shore
While minnows tease my toes, dart out of reach
And time slows down, and I need nothing more.

The warm dream freezes in the winter weather.
I stand and stretch, and fetch another sweater.

Timing
Late spring

Can this small patch of earth where I
plant my impatiens dirt caked under nails
ground into knees be the spot that just three
months thirteen weeks ninety days earlier hid
deep under cover out of reach glacier hard
while I shivered close by in boots parka gloves
watched my breath freeze clutched my shovel
dug a path strained my back cursed the snow?

If Time stopped stringing her moment to
moment spilled them out in cascades of
minutes months seconds years would I
find myself planting pinks and purples in
snowdrifts raking red gold orange leaves
off sunburnt summer grass celebrating Easter
under a harvest moon living dying singing
crying in a timeless crash of then soon and now?

But Time's hard pearls still tick into place on her
unending thread all order all sequence everything
in turn turn turn every season each lifetime as we
trip bead to bead powerless to pause to step back
see the whole as it winds out of sight out of mind
twisting and twining in astounding design so
precise it holds moment to moment lets me
plant pinks and purples not a snowflake in sight.

Eye of the beholder
Eastern Point, Nahant
Early spring

Morning light limns each branch
the dusting of soft fuzz glows neon bright
creates a spring halo, a nimbus of new growth
transfigures bare branches to burning bush

You pull out your cell, snap the shot
a crosshatch of naked sticks
glow gone, a trick of light
the camera cannot capture.

Normal

Weird percussion
clangs and crashes
screaming vocals
fill the living room
where he works on his math
pound into me
as I work in the kitchen.
I want to cover my ears.

I want to drink it in.
Normal sounds of a 17-year-old
when for years, a lifetime
so little was normal.

Wave

Seawall, Lynn

It races forward
dark and glassy
swells with power
foams with white
pounds the seawall
thump and rumble
thunders upward
shakes the ground
races higher
slaps the railing
scrabbles up the empty air
turns to downpour
smacks the pavement
briny rainfall drenches me.

I laugh.

Magnolia

I look for you each morning
walk past a riot of blooms
on your overdressed neighbors

Your spare beauty arrests me
a scatter of pink blossoms
pale hands cupped heavenward

I will remember your stillness
before petals flutter down
prayer forgotten.

The college years
a mother's running prayer

I can't let go yet, can't be free because
please help him please help him
he can't run his world can't handle life
help him please he needs help
so he calls and cries and wails and
please God just help him please
pours out his anguish in wave after wave
I'll do anything please help him
of hissed insults and "shut ups" and hang ups
just help him please God I can't
knowing I'll call back, knowing he can count
help him I'm begging you help him
on me, always me, only me, to absorb his pain
help him are you listening? please
listen to his misery scramble to find
help him are you there? God help
help but it's not enough never enough
help him help me God just help

Lawn musings

There's something about a fresh-mown lawn
that's lifeless.
Tiny stalks, crew-cut, edged square
rows of unmoving, green-uniformed troops
ignoring the breeze that ruffles above them
straight, stiff, unyielding.

It makes me wonder if
blades of grass dream
of a mower-free world
where snakes of air ripple
through honey-gold prairie grass
send stalks into spins and twirls
dancing waves of shadow and light
grass, wind, sun, rain, nothing more.

They can move to my yard
where mower blades rust
and grass can grow free.

Wild cherries

Stumpy trunked, rough skinned
splay-branched dwarves
who usually know their place.
Nothing like their stately sisters
graceful, serene, in fresh spring green.

But then comes dress-up time
when they whip out the wild hair.

Fat blooms pile bouffant high
punked-out pink spiking through
dreadlocks drip bubblegum blossoms
for the stylists to sweep
flashy falls, wild weaves, fuchsia flips—
they've got it all.

For two short weeks they're in the pink
till, spring fever burned out
they settle down for summer
and behave.

Just as you ought to be

Oh, Jesse, you ain't happy
I know that you ain't happy
I wish you could be happy
That's all that I want for thee.

Please try to sing, dear
Know that you're one who's wonderful
Please lighten up, dear
You're just as you ought to be.

I wish you'd let yourself know
The world, it has a place for you
I wish you'd let yourself go
And be who you want to be.

Please try to dance, dear
Don't try to hide, don't run away
Please take the chance, dear
You might find yourself set free.

I wish you'd see through my eyes
How beautiful you really are
I wish you knew what I know
You're just who you ought to be.

Second skin
To my son

I breathe it, eat it
sip it with my morning coffee
wear it like a second skin.

This bond, this link
this you in me
makes my heart leap
when your mind leaps past mine
yanks me down
when you crash and burn
blackens my world
when yours goes gray
raises my hope to dizzy heights
when I glimpse where you might go.

I know I must
cut those ties
cast you off
watch you pull ahead
and out of my sight.
I just don't know how.

Constant prayer

I have no idea who I pray to
yet still I do, toss up prayers
like confetti, like St. Francis
releasing his birds of the air
to fly who knows where.

I pray all the time anyplace
on request, "pray for me"
can't hurt, here goes nothing
by myself in the dark
help my life, please be real.

I don't expect an answer
really, half-belief at best
my fuel, yet still the words
form in my heart, spill out
the need to pray so strong.

Then through dark glass
I glimpse a hint of more
than mere coincidence
and I wonder if a prayer
at last has found its home...

Imagine

...that kid at the edge of the playground
who twirls like a top during recess
eyes closed, jacket flying, ignoring the
skip-roping, sand-digging, see-sawing masses
an apprentice magician casting her first spell.

...that pair of nutty girls, oblivious to stickball
and tag games swirling around them as they
sail the front porch down a rustling river
of autumn leaves blowing by in the breeze
wooden rail saving them from tumbling into the
rushing Amazon, where schools of piranha fish
munch through their hull to have them for lunch.

...the dreamer slouched in the back of the class
reading *The Two Towers* under her desk
lost deep in Fangorn with Merry and Pippin
whose hand shoots up to talk of *The Tempest*
but doesn't speak calculus.

But the muscle grows weak from years of neglect
underused, sapped of strength by ordinary and boring
dishes and school pickups, bills and car repairs
bludgeoned to numbness by fear and idiocy
hate crimes and genocide, politics and *Real Housewives*.
It becomes hard to picture anything beyond
this too, too solid world.

So here's the rub: I want to believe in spite of it all.
In mystery, spirit, the Oversoul, a world beyond this.

Imagine with me, believe with me, and make it true.

Word salad

In the pile of scrap
on the back of a page
the dregs of ink:

*Chinese man. Little do
her forties, her German
Egypt once...
"Because of money, and"
she said "women."
"Why?" she asked
a foreigner.
Pine trees whizzed by
our hotel landing.*

More faintly:
*two meals a day
attract a Chinese lover
Marika, who exuded worldly
school teaching.
An artist at her college
of money, and a foreigner,
mixed with trees red, orange,
over waters rushing pellmell
tea tables, chairs, cupboards, cups and—*

You page through the pile
but find nothing.
You strain to read
but the lines fade out.
You want to learn more
of this fever dream land

Of worldly Marika
and the Chinese lover
the flying pines...

What about the artist
the money school
that pesky foreigner
the flaming trees?
Did they all drown?

And the tea tables and cups
all left hanging—

CPSIA information can be obtained at www.ICGtesting.com
Printed in the USA
BVOW080423280513

321688BV00001B/2/P